TOP SECRET

SECRET

SILENT
WEAPONS
FOR
QUIET
WARS

D1551280

CONFIDENTIAL

Originally publication date unknown
circa 1954, 1969 or 1979
by what seems to be a
U. S. government agency or contractor,
unknown by name
OR, as claimed in 1996
Lyle Hartford Van Dyke
who failed to copyright

previous Book Tree printing 1998

ISBN 978-1-58509-380-9

background cover art
© imagestockdesign

Cover layout
Paul Tice

Published by
The Book Tree
P O Box 16476
San Diego, CA 92176
www.thebooktree.com

We provide fascinating and educational products to help awaken the public to new ideas and
information that would not be available otherwise.
Call 1 (800) 700-8733 for our *FREE BOOK TREE CATALOG*.

INTRODUCTION

This booklet has been considered to be true and legitimate in every way by those in the "conspiracy" community for quite some time. It has a rather compelling story of having been discovered wedged inside a copier machine that was purchased at a government-related surplus sale in 1986.

It is now believed by many that the compiler of this document is one Lyle Hartford Van Dyke, who claims to have assembled it from multiple sources (admitted for the first time, according to him, on a talk radio show in 1996). In an earlier edition of this booklet, which we reprinted in 1998, we were unaware of Mr. Van Dyke and his claims. This work may well have been assembled by Van Dyke after being written by government-related workers or an agency, and combined with other sources. However, questions still remain. It has been reported on the Internet that Mr. Van Dyke is a convicted felon and had spent time in jail. He claims that his run-ins with the law happened, in part, because of *Silent Weapons for Quiet Wars* and other works.

In a detailed letter written from federal prison to Paranoia Magazine in 2003, in response to a related article, he states that the book is not a hoax. He claims to have studied and used many different, relevant sources to arrive at "a politically biased technical instruction manual on how to justify, and how to selectively survive, human animal husbandry before the need for animal husbandry becomes unstably critical.... It is not a 'hoax' any more than any other presentation of a scientific process could be deemed a hoax merely because it was not presented with the endorsement of its original discoverer. SWFQW has many authors." He called it "...a collage, an overlay and paste-up of the works and words of many authors. I was the author only in the sense that I compiled and linked the gems of other writers."

Should this be the case, many are thankful. Van Dyke claims to have published this in December of 1979 after working on it for over a year. Just how much that was assembled by him is still an issue. William Cooper mentions *SWFQW* in his well-known book, *Behold a Pale Horse*, where he reproduces it and comments upon it. Cooper was a former Naval Intelligence Officer who had access to Top Secret material. He states, "I read Top Secret documents which explains that *Silent Weapons for Quiet Wars* is the doctrine adopted by the Policy Committee of the Bilderberg Group during its first known meeting in 1954. A copy found in 1969 was in the possession of Naval Intelligence."

So Cooper claims that it was *not* first assembled in 1979, but existed as early as 1954, for the purpose of its stated intention, and that a copy was in possession of Naval Intelligence in 1969, ten years earlier than Van Dyke claims to have compiled it. Cooper reproduced in *Behold a Pale Horse* a copy of the 1979 document, which included the "Welcome Aboard" page that conforms to a 1979 "creation." So this 1979 version could easily be what Van Dyke assembled—but how much of it is still in question.

At the end his own reprinting, Cooper says, "The document, first found in 1969, correctly outlines events which subsequently came to pass. It cannot be ignored or dismissed. The document is genuine. Its truths cannot be negated or shrugged away." Cooper is referring to the veracity of the information as opposed to authorship, but the repeated 1969 date points to the Naval Intelligence copy that he had previously mentioned, and existed at that time.

Was Lyle Van Dyke just seeking attention, and knowing that no legitimate source would ever step forward and take credit for it, he decided to? He was convicted of fraud in 2003 (for trying to pass $3 million in false currency, according to the Associated Press, 7/30/2003), so I'm sorry, but his background raises some issues. His argument is still worth considering because his situation could give one cause to assemble such a work. So hats off to Van Dyke if he indeed put all this together. We cannot rule it out, but serious questions arise.

Bill Cooper, now deceased, reportedly had issues of his own, including problems with alcohol. So who do we believe? Bill Cooper—who claimed knowledge of an earlier edition that was apparently strong enough to base policy from? Or Lyle Van Dyke—who claims to have put it all together in 1978-1979? Or neither one?

Van Dyke had trouble with the law, so one must wonder if a deal was struck. Was his attribution created with government involvement, to shift blame away, based on Cooper's knowledge of earlier "editions?" Could a government agency have recruited Van Dyke (after *SWFQW* was found in 1986) to remove a potential embarrassment? This idea may be nothing more than a fanciful conspiracy theory (within a conspiracy theory), but Van Dyke's background begs the question. He cannot account for any copies he claims to have made between 1979 to 1986—except for (possibly) the one found in the copier, which he claims was given to a random, unknown military hitchhiker whom he dropped off at an Air Force Base.

William Cooper had access to secret documents and vouched for this document's existence before Van Dyke came along. There is also Delamer Deverus, who apparently received a copy of the 1979 version before passing it along to Cooper. Deverus' assessment was as follows:

"I can assure you that the manual is authentic, and was printed for the purpose of introducing the selectee to the conspiracy. It has been authenticated by four different technical writers for Military Intelligence, one just recently retired who wants very much to have this manual distributed throughout the world, and one who is still employed as an Electronics Engineer by the Federal Government, and has access to the entire series of Training Manuals. One was stationed in Hawaii, and held the highest security clearance in the Naval Intelligence, and another who is now teaching at a university, and has been working with the Central Intelligence Agency for a number of years,..."

Since we're referring to the 1979 version, all these people got this document after Van Dyke had apparently assembled it. Good for him. But could Van Dyke have added a little less to a larger document, which could account for the earlier reports? There are numerous links and documents which support Van Dykes' claims, however, available on-line to explore.

Wherever it came from, it is the content of this document that is most intriguing. It refers to things that many say have come to pass, so makes interesting reading. Yes, many should be grateful to Lyle Van Dyke should he have been the person to assemble it. We don't rule it out. At the same time, any reasonable person cannot help but to continue to question its source (or sources). A good dose of healthy skepticism is always a good thing within the field on conspiracy.

With all being said, and the waters remaining muddy, we leave it to the reader to form their own opinions regarding authorship and the legitimacy of the plan which the book contains. With all things considered, we do not name an author for this work, as was clearly the original intention with its first release, and as reflected in our earlier 1998 edition. Whatever path this work has taken, it seems clear that multiple contributors were involved. We therefore leave such things open for the reader to determine—and to form an opinion.

The main truth is that this document exists. We ask that you explore things further, test the legitimacy of this work, and form whatever opinions that you may.

This version is reprinted in its original form, complete with the important diagrams which are not included in digital versions found elsewhere. The print quality is lacking on some pages, but reflects the original accurately, as it was found. The only differences one may see are a few minor, hand-corrected mistakes, or the filling in of omitted words, or partial words, for the sake of accuracy.

What follows is the Preface from the previous edition, unsigned by its author. It could be the words of Van Dyke, or those of a previous publisher. Now that it follows this Introduction, it is felt that one can read it in a better context—along with the complete book, which follows.

Paul Tice

PREFACE

Conspiracy theories are nothing new to history. Plots to "kill Caesar" and overthrow Rome abounded, for instance. However, it is seldom that concrete clues to such plots come to light, and are generally known.

The document you are about to read is real. It is no forgery, as alleged of *The Protocols of the Learned Elders of Zion*, or actual forgeries such as those of Anne Frank, or (more recently) Hitler's diary.

TOP SECRET: Silent Weapons for Quiet Wars, An Introductory Programming Manual was uncovered quite by accident on July 7, 1986 when an employee of Boeing Aircraft Company purchased a surplus IBM copier for scrap parts at a sale, and discovered inside details of a plan, hatched in the embryonic days of the "Cold War," which called for control of the masses through manipulation of industry, peoples' pasttimes, education and political leanings. It called for a quiet revolution, putting brother against brother, and diverting the public's attention from what is really going on.

For all intents and purposes, this document has "come to pass," much as Henry Ford, Sr. said that the *Protocols* (regardless of their veracity) applied to the events of his day.

It is reprinted in its virgin form, with diagrams, as a touch of reality.

It is heavy reading, but it will (as it well should) spur you to read further, keep your eyes and ears open, and sound an alarm in Zion, for though she presently dwells with Babylon's daughter (Micah 4), her redemption draweth nigh.

Truth bears no fear.

—— TOP SECRET ——

SILENT WEAPONS
FOR QUIET WARS

An introductory
programing manual.

OPERATIONS RESEARCH
TECHNICAL MANUAL
TM-SW7905.1

Technical Manual No. SW7905.1 — SILENT WEAPONS FOR QUIET WARS

TABLE OF CONTENTS

SECURITY

It is patently impossible to discuss social engineering or the automation of a society, i.e., the engineering of social automation systems (silent weapons) on a national or worldwide scale without implying extensive objectives of social control and destruction of human life, i.e., slavery and genocide.

This manual is in itself an analog declaration of intent. Such a writing must be secured from public scrutiny. Otherwise, it might be recognized as a technically formal declaration of domestic war. Furthermore, whenever any person or group of persons in a position of great power, and without the full knowledge and consent of the public, uses such knowledge and methodology for economic conquest — it must be understood that a state of domestic warfare exists between said person or group of persons and the public.

The solution of today's problems requires an approach which is ruthlessly candid, with no agonizing over religious, moral, or cultural values.

You have qualified for this project because of your ability to look at human society with cold objectivity, and yet analyze and discuss your observations and conclusions with others of similar intellectual capacity without a loss of discretion or humility.

Such virtues are exercised in
your own best interest.
Do not deviate from them.

4

WELCOME ABOARD

This publication marks the 25th anniversary
of the Third World War, called the 'Quiet War',
being conducted using subjective biological warfare, fought with 'silent weapons'.

This book contains an introductory description
of this war, its strategies, and its weaponry.

May 1979   #74-1120

HISTORICAL INTRODUCTION

Silent weapon technology has evolved from Operations Research (O.R.), a strategic and tactical methodology developed under the military management in England during World War II. The original purpose of Operations Research was to study the strategic and tactical problems of air and land defense with the objective of effective use of limited military resources against foreign enemies (i.e., logistics).

It was soon recognized by those in positions of power that the same methods might be useful for totally controling a society. But better tools were necessary.

Social engineering (the analysis and automation of a society) requires the correlation of great amounts of constantly changing economic information (data), so a high speed computerized data processing system was necessary which could race ahead of the society and predict when society would arrive for capitulation.

Relay computers were too slow, but the electronic computer, invented in 1946 by J. Presper Eckert and John W. Mauchly filled the bill.

The next breakthrough was the development of the simplex method of linear programing in 1947 by the mathematician George B. Dantzig.

Then, in 1948, the transistor, invented by J. Bardeen, W. H. Brattain, and W. Shockley, promised great expansion of the computer field by reducing space and power requirements.

With these three inventions under their direction, those in positions of power strongly suspected that it was possible for them to control the whole world with the push of a button.

Immediately, the Rockefeller Foundation got in on the ground floor by making a four year grant to Harvard College, funding the Harvard economic research project for the study of the structure of the American economy. One year later, in 1949, the United States Air Force joined in.

In 1952 the original grant period terminated, and a high level meeting of the elite was held to determine the next phase of social operations research. The Harvard project had been very fruitful as is borne out by the publication of some of its results in 1953 suggesting the feasibility of economic (social) engineering. (Studies in the Structure of the American Economy -- copyright 1953 by Wassily Leontief, International Sciences Press Inc., White Plains, New York.)

Engineered in the last half decade of the 1940's, the new Quiet War machine stood, so to-speak, in sparkling gold plated hardware on the showroom floor by 1954.

With the creation of the maser in 1954, the promise of unlocking unlimited sources of fusion atomic energy from the heavy hydrogen in sea water and the consequent availability of unlimited social power became a possibility only decades away.

The combination was irresistible.

The Quiet War was quietly declared by the international elite at a meeting held in 1954.

Although the silent weapons system was nearly exposed 13 years later, the evolution of the new weapon system has never suffered any major setbacks.

This volume marks the 25th anniversary of the beginning of the Quiet War. Already this domestic war has had many victories on many fronts throughout the world.

POLITICAL INTRODUCTION

In 1954 it was well recognized by those in positions of authority that it was only a matter of time, only a few decades, before the general public would be able to grasp and upset the cradle of power, for the very elements of the new silent weapon technology were as accessable for a public utopia as they were for providing a private utopia.

The issue of primary concern, that of dominance, revolved around the subject of the energy sciences.

ENERGY

Energy is recognized as the key to all activity on earth. Natural science is the study of the sources and control of natural energy, and social science, theoretically expressed as economics, is the study of the sources and control of social energy. Both are bookkeeping systems: mathematics. Therefore, mathematics is the primary energy science. And the bookkeeper can be king if the public can be kept ignorant of the methodology of the bookkeeping.

All science is merely a means to an end. The means is knowledge. The end is control. Beyond this remains only one issue, "who will be the beneficiary?".

In 1954 this was the issue of primary concern. Although the so-called "moral issues" were raised, in view of the law of natural selection it was agreed that a nation or world of people who will not use their intelligence are no better than animals who do not have intelligence. Such a people are beasts of burden and steaks on the table by choice and consent.

CONSEQUENTLY, in the interest of future world order, peace, and tranquility, it was decided to privately wage a quiet war against the American public with an ultimate objective of permanently shifting the natural and social energy (wealth) of the undisciplined and irresponsible many into the hands of the self-disciplined, responsible, and worthy few.

In order to implement this objective, it was necessary to create, secure, and apply new weapons which, as it turned out, were a class of weapons so subtle and sophisticated in their principle of operation and public appearance as to earn for themselves the name 'silent weapons'.

In conclusion, the objective of economic research, as conducted by the magnates of capital (banking) and the industries of commodities(goods) and services, is the establishment of an economy which is totally predictable and manipulatable.

In order to achieve a totally predictable economy, the low class elements of the society must be brought under total control, i.e., must be house-broken, trained, and assigned a yoke and long term social duties from a very early age, before they have an opportunity to question the propriety of the matter. In order to achieve such conformity, the lower class family unit must be disintegrated by a process of increasing preoccupation of the parents and the establishment of government operated day care centers for the occupationally orphaned children.

The quality of education given to the lower class must be of the poorest sort, so that the moat of ignorance isolating the inferior class from the superior class is and remains incomprehensible to the inferior class. With such an initial handicap, even bright lower class individuals have little if any hope of extricating themselves from their assigned lot in life. This form of slavery is essential to maintaining some measure of social order, peace, and tranquility for the ruling upper class.

DESCRIPTIVE INTRODUCTION
OF THE SILENT WEAPON

Everything that is expected from an ordinary weapon is expected from a silent weapon by its creators, but only in its own manner of functioning.

It shoots situations, instead of bullets; propelled by data processing, instead of a chemical reaction (explosion); originating from bits of data, instead of grains of gunpowder; from a computer, instead of a gun; operated by a computer programer, instead of a marksman; under the orders of a banking magnate, instead of a military general.

It makes NO ~~to~~ obvious explosive noises, causes
no obvious physical or mental injuries, and does
not obviously interfere with anyone's daily social
life.

Yet it makes an unmistakable 'noise', causes
unmistakable physical and mental damage, and un-
mistakably interferes with daily social life, i.e.
unmistakable to a trained observer, one who knows
what to look for.

The public cannot comprehend this weapon, and
therefore cannot believe that they are being
attacked and subdued by a weapon.

The public might instinctively feel that
something is wrong, but because of the technical
nature of the silent weapon, they cannot express
their feeling in a rational way, or handle the
problem with intelligence. Therefore, they do not
know how to cry for help, and do not know how to
associate with others to defend themselves against it.

When a silent weapon is applied gradually to
the public, the public adjusts/adapts to its presence
and learns to tolerate its encroachment on their
lives until the pressure (psychological via economic) becomes too great and they crack up.

Therefore, the silent weapon is a type of biological warfare. It attacks the vitality, options,
and mobility of the individuals of a society by
knowing, understanding, manipulating, and attacking
their sources of natural and social energy, and
their physical, mental, and emotional strengths and
weaknesses.

THEORETICAL INTRODUCTION

"Give me control over a nation's currency,
and I care not who makes its laws."
Mayer Amschel Rothschild (1743-1812)

Today's silent weapons technology is an out-
growth of a simple idea discovered, succinctly
expressed, and effectively applied by the quoted

Mr. Mayer Amschel Rothschild. Mr. Rothschild
discovered the missing passive component of economic
theory known as economic inductance. He, of course,
did not think of his discovery in these 20th century
terms, and, to be sure, mathematical analysis had to
wait for the Second Industrial Revolution, the rise
of the theory of mechanics and electronics, and
finally, the invention of the electronic computer
before it could be effectively applied in the control
of the world economy.

GENERAL ENERGY CONCEPTS

In the study of energy systems, there always
appear three elementary concepts. These are potential energy, kinetic energy, and energy dissipation.
And corresponding to these concepts, there are three
idealized, essentially pure physical counterparts,
called passive components.

(1) In the science of physical mechanics, the
phenomenon of potential energy is associated with a
physical property called elasticity or stiffness,
and can be represented by a stretched spring.

In electronic science, potential energy is stored
in a capacitor instead of a spring. This property
is called capacitance instead of elasticity or
stiffness.

(2) In the science of physical mechanics, the
phenomenon of kinetic energy is associated with a
physical property called inertia or mass and can
be represented by a mass or a flywheel in motion.

In electronic science, kinetic energy is stored
in an inductor (in a magnetic field) instead of a
mass. This property is called inductance instead
of inertia.

(3) In the science of physical mechanics, the phenomenon of energy dissipation is associated with a physical property called friction or resistance. and can be represented by a dashpot or other device which converts system energy into heat.

In electronic science, dissipation of energy is performed by an element called either a resistor or a conductor, the term 'resistor' being the one generally used to express the concept of friction, and the term 'conductor' being generally used to describe a more ideal device (e.g., wire) employed to convey electric energy efficiently from one location to another. The property of a resistance or conductor is measured as either resistance or conductance, reciprocals.

In economics these three energy concepts are associated with:
  (1) Economic Capacitance -- Capital (money, stock/inventory, investments in buildings and durables, etc.)
  (2) Economic Conductance -- Goods (production flow coefficients)
  (3) Economic Inductance -- Services (the influence of the population of industry on output)

All of the mathematical theory developed in the study of one energy system, (e.g., mechanics, electronics, etc.) can be immediately applied in the study of any other energy system (e.g., economics).

MR. ROTHSCHILD'S ENERGY DISCOVERY

What Mr. Rothschild had discovered was the basic principle of power. influence, and control over people as applied to economics. That principle is "when you assume the appearance of power, people soon give it to you".

12

Mr. Rothschild had discovered that currency
or deposit loan accounts had the required appearance of power that could be used to induce people
(inductance, with people corresponding to a
magnetic field) into surrendering their real wealth
in exchange for a promise of greater wealth (instead of real compensation). They would put up
real colateral in exchange for a loan of promisory
notes. Mr. Rothschild found that he could issue
more notes than he had backing for, so long as he
had someone's stock of gold as a persuader to show
to his customers.

Mr. Rothschild loaned his promisory notes to
individuals and to governments. These would create
over-confidence. Then he would make money scarce,
tighten control of the system, and collect the
colateral through the obligation of contracts. The
cycle was then repeated. These pressures could be
used to ignite a war. Then he would control the
availability of currency to determine who would win
the war. That government which agreed to give him
control of its economic system got his support.
Collection of debts was guaranteed by economic aid
to the enemy of the debtor. The profit derived
from this economic methodology made Mr. Rothschild
all the more wealthy and all the more able to
extend his wealth. He found that the public greed
would allow currency to be printed by government
order beyond the limits (inflation) of backing in
precious metal or the production of goods and services (gross national product, GNP).

APPARENT CAPITAL AS
"PAPER" INDUCTOR

In this structure, credit, presented as a
pure circuit element called "currency", has the
appearance of capital, but is, in fact, negative
capital. Hence, it has the appearance of service,
but is, in fact, indebtedness or debt. It is therefore an economic inductance instead of an economic
capacitance, and if balanced in no other way, will

be balanced by the negation of population (war, genocide). The total goods and services represents real capital called the gross national product, and currency may be printed up to this level and still represent economic capacitance; but currency printed beyond this level is subtractive, represents the introduction of economic inductance, and constitutes notes of indebtedness. War is therefore the balancing of the system by killing the true creditors (the public which we have taught to exchange true value for inflated currency) and falling back on whatever is left of the resources of nature and the regeneration of those resources.

Mr. Rothschild had discovered that currency gave him the power to rearrange the economic structure to his own advantage, to shift economic inductance to those economic positions which would encourage the greatest economic instability and oscillation.

The final key to economic control had to wait until there was sufficient data and high speed computing equipment to keep close watch on the economic oscillations created by price shocking and excess paper energy credits.— (paper inductance/inflation).

BREAKTHROUGH

The aviation field provided the greatest evolution in economic engineering by way of the mathematical theory of shock testing. In this process, a projectile is fired from an airframe on the ground and the impulse of the recoil is monitored by vibration transducers connected to the airframe and wired to chart recorders. By studying the echoes or reflections of the recoil impulse in the airframe, it is possible to discover critical vibrations in the structure of the airframe which either vibrations of the engine or aeolian vibrations of the wings, or a combination of the two, might reinforce resulting in a resonant self-destruction of the airframe in flight as an aircraft. From the standpoint of engineering, this means that the

14

strengths and weaknesses of the structure of the
airframe in terms of vibrational energy can be
discovered and manipulated.

APPLICATION IN ECONOMICS

To use this method of airframe shock testing
in economic engineering, the prices of commodities
are shocked, and the public consumer reaction is
monitored. The resulting echoes of the economic
shock are interpreted theoretically by computers
and the psycho-economic structure of the economy
is thus discovered. It is by this process that
partial differential and difference matrices are
discovered that define the family household and
make possible its evaluation as an economic industry (disaipitive consumer structure). Then the
response of the household to future shocks can be
predicted and manipulated, and society becomes a
well regulated animal with its reins under the
control of a sophisticated computer-regulated
social energy bookkeeping system.

Eventually every individual element of the
structure comes under computer control through a
knowledge of personal preferences, such knowledge
guaranteed by computer association of consumer
preferences (universal product code -- UPC --
zebra stripe pricing codes on packages) with
identified consumers (identified via association
with the use of a credit card and later a perma-
nent 'tatooed' body number invisible under normal
ambient illumination.

SUMMARY

Economics is only a social extension of a
natural energy system. It, also, has its three
passive components. Because of the distribution
of wealth and the lack of communication and
consequent lack of data, this field has been the
last energy field for which a knowledge of these

three passive components has been developed.

Since energy is the key to all activity on the face of the earth, it follows that in order to attain a monopoly of energy, raw materials, goods, and services and to establish a world system of slave labor, it is necessary to have a first strike capability in the field of economics. In order to maintain our position, it is necessary that we have absolute first knowledge of the science of control over all economic factors and the first experience at engineering the world economy.

In order to achieve such sovereignty, we must at least achieve this one end: that the public will not make either the logical or mathematical connection between economics and the other energy sciences or learn to apply such knowledge.

This is becoming increasingly difficult to control because more and more businesses are making demands upon their computer programers to create and apply mathematical models for the management of those businesses.

It is only a matter of time before the new breed of private programer/economists will catch on to the far reaching implications of the work begun at Harvard in 1948. The speed with which they can communicate their warning to the public will largely depend upon how effective we have been at controling the media, subverting education and keeping the public distracted with matters of no real importance.

THE ECONOMIC MODEL

Economics, as a social energy science has as a first objective the description of the complex way in which any given unit of resources is used to satisfy some economic want. (Leontief Matrix) This first objective, when it is extended to get the most product from the least or limited resources, comprises that objective of general military and industrial logistics known as Operations Research.(See simplex method of linear programing.)

The Harvard Economic Research Project (1948-) was an extension of World War II Operations Research. Its purpose was to discover the science of controling an economy: at first the American economy, and then the world economy. It was felt that with sufficient mathematical foundation and data, it would be nearly as easy to predict and control the trend of an economy as to predict and control the trajectory of a projectile. Such has proven to be the case. Moreover, the economy has been transformed into a guided missile on target.

The immediate aim of the Harvard project was to discover the economic structure, what forces change that structure, how the behavior of the structure can be predicted, and how it can be manipulated. What was needed was a well organized knowledge of the mathematical structures and interrelationships of investment, production, distribution, and consumption. To make a short story of it all, it was discovered that an economy obeyed the same laws as electricity and that all of the mathematical theory and practical and computer know-how developed for the electronic field could be directly applied in the study of economics. This discovery was not openly declared, and its more subtle implications were and are kept a closely guarded secret, for example that in an economic model, human life is measured in dollars, and that the electric spark generated when opening a switch connected to an active inductor is mathematically analogous to the initiation of a war.

The greatest hurdle which theoretical economists
faced was the accurate description of the household
as an industry. This is a challenge, because consumer purchases are a matter of choice which in turn
is influenced by income, price, and other economic
factors.

This hurdle was cleared in an indirect and
statistically approximate way by an application of
shock testing to determine the current characteristics, called current technical coefficients, of
a household industry.

Finally, because problems in theoretical
economics can be translated very easily into problems in theoretical electronics, and the solution
translated back again, it follows that only a book
of language translation and concept definition
needed to be written for economics. The remainder
could be gotten from standard works on mathematics
and electronics. This makes the publication of
books on advanced economics unnecessary, and greatly
simplifies project security.

INDUSTRIAL DIAGRAMS

An ideal industry is defined as a device which
receives value from other industries in several forms
and converts it into one specific product for sales
and distribution to other industries. It has
several inputs and one output. What the public nor-
mally thinks of as one industry is really an industrial complex where several industries under one
roof produce one or more products.

A pure (single output) industry can be represented oversimply by a circuit block as follows.

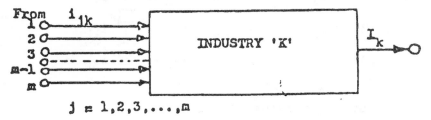

$$j = 1,2,3,\ldots,m$$

The flow of product from industry #1 (supply) to industry #2 (demand) is denoted by i_{12}. The total flow out of industry 'K' is denoted by I_k. (sales, etc.)

A three industry network can be diagramed as follows.

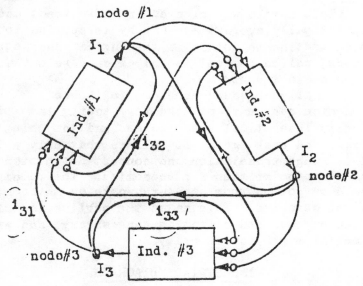

A node is a symbol of collection and distribution of flow. Node #3 receives from industry #3 and distributes to industries #1 through #3. If industry #3 manufactures chairs, then a flow from industry #3 back to industry #3 simply indicates that industry #3 is using part of its own output product, for example, as office furniture. Therefore the flow may be summarized by the equations:

Node #1 : $I_1 = i_{11} + i_{12} + i_{13} = \sum i_{1k}$

Node #2 : $I_2 = i_{21} + i_{22} + i_{23} = \sum i_{2k}$

Node #3 : $I_3 = i_{31} + i_{32} + i_{33} = \sum i_{3k}$

where $\sum$ denotes $\sum_{k=1}^{k=3}$

THREE INDUSTRIAL CLASSES

Industries fall into three categories or classes by type of output.

Class #1 - Capital (resources)
Class #2 - Goods (commodities or use - dissipative)
Class #3 - Services (action of population)

Class #1 industries exist at three levels
  (1) Nature- sources of energy and raw materials.
  (2) Government- printing of currency equal to gross national product (GNP), and extension*of currency in excess of GNP.
  (3) Banking- loaning of money for interest, and extension*(counterfeiting) of economic value through deposit loan accounts.
      *- inflation.
Class #2 industries exist as producers of tangible or consumer (dissipated) products. This sort of activity is usually recognized and labeled by the public as an 'industry'.
Class #3 industries are those which have service rather than a tangible product as their output. These industries are called (1) households, and (2) governments. Their output is human activity of a mechanical sort, and their basis is population.

AGGREGATION

The whole economic system can be represented by a three industry model if one allows the names of the outputs to be (1) capital, (2) goods, and (3) services. The problem with this representation is that it would not show the influence of, say, the textile industry on the ferrous metal industry. This is because both the textile industry and the ferrous metal industry would be contained within a single classification called the 'goods industry', and by this process of combining or aggregating those two industries under one system block they would lose their economic individuality.

THE E-MODEL

A national economy consists of simultaneous flows of production, distribution, consumption, and investment. If all of these elements including labor and human functions are assigned a numerical value in like units of measure, say, 1939 dollars, then this flow can be further represented by a current flow in an electronic circuit, and its behavior can be predicted and manipulated with useful precision.

The three ideal passive energy components of electronics, the capacitor, the resistor, and the inductor correspond to the three ideal passive energy components of economics called the pure industries of capital, goods, and services, resp..

Economic capacitance represents the storage of capital in one form or another.

Economic conductance represents the level of conductance of materials for the production of goods.

Economic inductance represents the inertia of economic value in motion. This is a population phenomenon known as services.

ECONOMIC INDUCTANCE

An electrical inductor (e.g., a coil of wire) has an electric current as its primary phenomenon and a magnetic field as its secondary phenomenon (inertia). Corresponding to this, an economic inductor has a flow of economic value as its primary phenomenon and a population field as its secondary phenomenon of inertia. When the flow of economic value (e.g., money) diminishes, the human population field collapses in order to keep the economic value (money) flowing (extreme case- war).

This public inertia is a result of consumer buying habits, expected standard of living, etc., and is generally a phenomenon of self-preservation.

INDUCTIVE FACTORS TO CONSIDER

(1) population
(2) magnitude of the economic activities of the government.
(3) the method of financing these government activities (see Peter-Paul Principle -- inflation of the currency)

TRANSLATION

(A few examples will be given.)
CHARGE-- coulombs-- dollars (1939).
FLOW/CURRENT -- amperes (coulombs per second).
                -- dollars of flow per year.
MOTIVATING FORCE -- volts -- dollars(output)demand.
CONDUCTANCE -- amperes per volt.
                -- dollars of flow per year per dollar demand.
CAPACITANCE -- coulombs per volt.
                -- dollars of production inventory/stock per dollar demand.

TIME-FLOW RELATIONSHIPS AND SELF-DESTRUCTIVE OSCILLATIONS

An ideal industry may be symbolized electronically in various ways. The simplest way is to represent a demand by a voltage and a supply by a current. When this is done, the relationship between the two becomes what is called an admittance, which can result from three economic factors: (1) hindsight flow, (2) present flow, and (3) foresight flow.

Foresight flow is the result of that property of living entities to cause energy (food) to be stored for a period of low energy (e.g., a winter season). It consists of demands made upon an economic system for that period of low energy (winter season). In a production industry it takes several forms, one of which is known as production stock or inventory. In electronic symbology this specific industry demand (a pure capital industry) is represented by capacitance and the stock or resource is represented by a stored charge. Satisfaction of an industry demand suffers a lag because of the loading effect of inventory priorities.

Present flow ideally involves no delays. It is, so to speak, input today for output today, a 'hand to mouth' flow. In electronic symbology, this specific industry demand (a pure use industry) is represented by a conductance which is then a simple economic valve (a dissipative element).

Hindsight flow is known as habit or inertia. In electronics, this phenomenon is the characteristic of an inductor (economic analog = a pure service industry) in which a current flow (economic analog = flow of money) creates a magnetic field (economic analog = active human population) which, if the current (money flow) begins to diminish, collapses (war) to maintain the current (flow of money--energy).

Other large alternatives to war as economic inductors or economic flywheels are an open-ended social welfare program, or enormous (but fruitful) open-ended space program.

The problem with stabilizing the economic system is that there is too much demand on account of (1) too much greed and (2) too much population.

This creates excessive economic inductance which can only be balanced with economic capacitance (true resources or value - e.g. in goods or services). The social welfare program is nothing more than an open-ended credit balance system which creates a false capital industry to give non-productive people a roof over their heads and food in their stomachs. This can be useful, how-

ever, because the recipients become state property
in return for the 'gift', a standing army for the
elite. For he who pays the piper, picks the tune.
Those who get hooked on the economic drug, must go
to the elite for a fix. In this, the method of
introducing large amounts of stabilizing capaci¢
tance is by borrowing on the future "credit" of the
world. This is a fourth law of motion -- onset,
and consists of performing an action and leaving
the system before the reflected reaction returns
to the point of action- a delayed reaction. The
means of surviving the reaction is by changing the
system before the reaction can return. By this
means, politicians become popular in their own
time and the public pays for it later. In fact
the measure of such a politician is the delay time.
The same thing is achieved by a government by
printing money beyond the limit of the gross
national product, an economic process called inflation. This puts a large quantity of money into
the hands of the public and maintains a balance
against their greed, creates a false self-
confidence in them and, for a while, stays the
wolf from the door.
        They must eventually resort to war to balance
the account, because war ultimately is merely the
act of destroying the creditor, and politicians
are the publicly hired hit men that justify the
act to keep the responsibility and blood off the
public conscience. (See section on consent factors
and social-economic structuring.)
        If the people really cared about their fellow
man, they would control their appetites (greed,
procreation, etc.) so that they would not have to
operate on a credit or welfare social system which
steals from the worker to satisfy the bum.
        Since most of the general public will not
exercise restraint, there are only two alternatives to reduce the economic inductance of the
system.
(1) Let the populace bludgeon each other to death
    in war, which will only result in a total
    destruction of the living earth.
(2) Take control of the world by the use of eco-

24

nomic 'silent weapons' in a form of 'quiet warfare',
and reduce the economic inductance of the world to
a safe level by a process of benevolent slavery and
genocide.

The latter option has been taken as the
obviously better option. At this point it should
be crystal clear to the reader why absolute secrecy
about the silent weapons is necessary. The general
public refuses to improve its own mentality and its
faith in its fellow man. It has become a herd of
proliferating barbarians, and, so to speak, a blight
upon the face of the earth. They do not care enough
about economic science to learn why they have not
been able to avoid war despite religious morality,
and their religious or self-gratifying refusal to
deal with earthly problems renders the solution of
the earthly problem unreachable by them. It is
left to those few who are truly willing to think
and survive as the fittest to survive, to solve the
problem for themselves as the few who really care.
Otherwise, exposure of the silent weapon would
destroy our only hope of preserving the seed of
future true humanity.

INDUSTRY EQUIVALENT CIRCUITS

The industry 'Q' can be given a block symbol as follows.

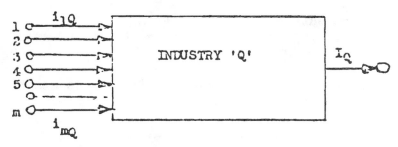

Block Diagram of Industry 'Q'.

Terminals #1 through #m are connected directly to the outputs of industries #1 through #m, resp..

The equivalent circuit of industry 'Q' is given as follows.

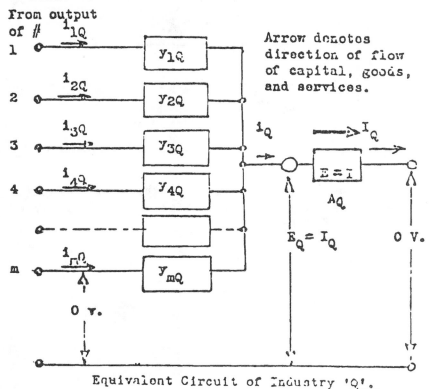

Equivalent Circuit of Industry 'Q'.

Characteristics;

All inputs are at zero volts.

A — Amplifier — causes output current X_Q to be
represented by a voltage E_Q. Amplifier delivers sufficient current at E_Q to drive all
loads y_{1Q} through y_{mQ} and sink all currents
i_{1Q} through i_{mQ}.

Tho unit transconductance amplifier A_Q is constr-
ucted as follows.

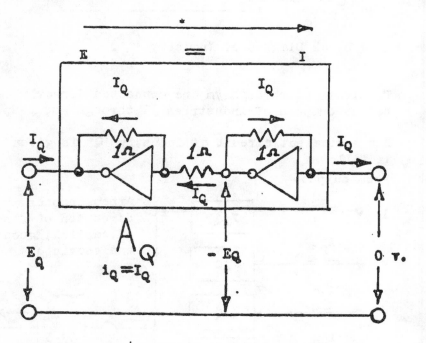

* Arrow denotes the direction of the flow of capital,
goods, and services. The total demand is given as
E_Q, where $E_Q = I_Q$.

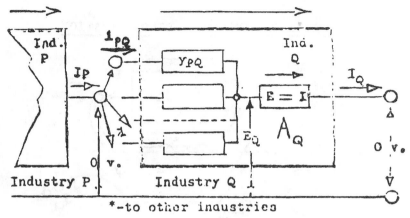

*-to other industries

The coupling network y_{PQ} symbolizes the demand which industry Q makes on industry P. The connective admittance y_{PQ} is called the 'technical coefficient' of the industry Q stating the demand of industry Q, called the industry of use, for the output in capital, goods, or services of industry P called the industry of origin.

The flow of commodities from industry P to industry Q is given by i_{PQ} evaluated by the formula

$$i_{PQ} = y_{PQ} \cdot E_Q .$$

When the admittance y_{PQ} is a simple conductance, this formula takes on the common appearance of Ohm's Law,

$$i_{PQ} = g_{PQ} \cdot E_Q .$$

The interconnection of a three industry system can be diagramed as follows. The blocks of the industry diagram can be opened up revealing the technical coefficients, and a much simpler format. The equations of flow are given as follows.

$$I_1 = i_{11} + i_{12} + i_{13} + i_{1o} = \sum i_{1k} + i_{1o}$$

$$I_2 = i_{21} + i_{22} + i_{23} + i_{2o} = \sum i_{2k} + i_{2o}$$

$$I_3 = i_{31} + i_{32} + i_{33} + i_{3o} = \sum i_{3k} + i_{3o}$$

STAGES OF SCHEMATIC SIMPLIFICATION

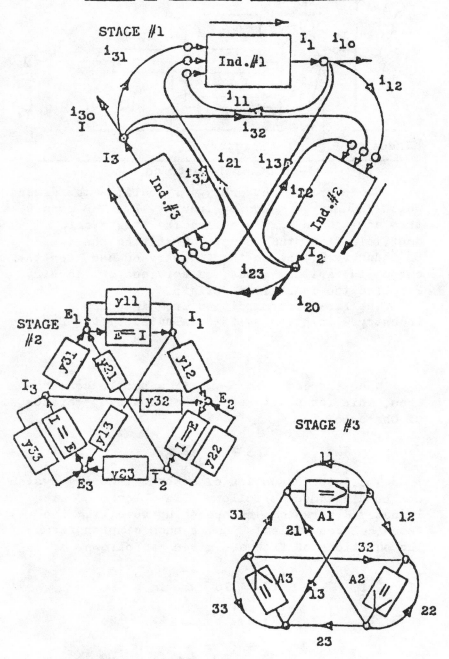

GENERALIZATION

All of this may now be summarized.

Let I_j represent the output of industry j, and

i_{jk}, the amount of the product of industry j absorbed annually by industry k, and

i_{jo}, the amount of the same product j made available for 'outside use'. Then

$$I_j = i_{j1} + i_{j2} + i_{j3} + \cdots + i_{jm} + i_{jo}$$

$$= \sum_{k=1}^{k=m} i_{jk} + i_{jo}$$

Substituting the technical coefficients, y_{jk}

$$i_{jk} = y_{jk} I_k$$

$$I_j = \sum_{k=1}^{k=m} i_{jk} + i_{jo} = \sum_{k=1}^{k=m} y_{jk} I_k + i_{jo}$$

Leontief Matrix for $j = 1,2,3,\ldots .m$
$$\left\{ I_j - \sum_{k=1}^{k=m} y_{jk} I_k = i_{jo} \right.$$

Let I_k at the output of industry k be represented by a demand voltage E_k at its amplifier input, i.e., let $E_k = I_k$. Then

$$i_{jk} = y_{jk} E_k$$

which is the general equation of every admittance in the industry circuit.

FINAL BILL OF GOODS

$$\sum_{j=1}^{j=m} i_{j0} = i_{10} + i_{20} + i_{30} + \cdots + i_{m0} \text{ is called}$$

the final bill of goods or the bill of final demand,
and is zero when the system can be closed by the
evaluation of the technical coefficients of the
'non-productive' industries, government and
households.   Households may be regarded as a
productive industry with labor as its output product.

THE TECHNICAL COEFFICIENTS

The quantities y_{jk} are called the technical
coefficients of the industrial system.   They are
admittances and can consist of any combination of
the three passive parameters, conductance, capacitance, and inductance.   Diodes are used to make
the flow unidirectional and point against the flow.

$\mathcal{E}_{jk}$ = economic conductance, absorption coefficient

C_{jk} = economic capacitance, capital coefficient

L_{jk} = economic inductance, human activity coeff.

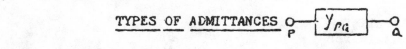

TYPES OF ADMITTANCES

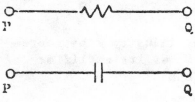

flow of product

storage in industry Q
of capital -- in the
form of inventory of
materials, stock of
equipment, work in
progress, intermediate
products,etc.. This
stock fully reversible
meaning that it can be
sold or exchanged for
other materials.

TYPES OF ADMITTANCES (CONT'D)

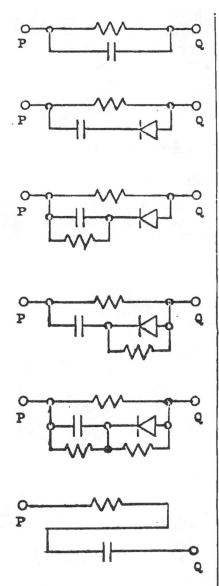

-flow and stock control,
stock is fully rever-
sible, e.g., can be
sold or exchanged for
other materials.
-flow, but stock not
reversible,
stock does not need
maintenance.

-here the stock is not
reversible, and it is
subject to depreciation.
- can also represent
capital tied up in
buildings which cannot
be sold and are aging.
-- here we have partially
reversible stock which
may be reversed at a
slower rate than it is
demanded during pro-
duction.
-here the stock rever-
sibility and depreci-
ation are accounted for.

- stock buildup is delayed
and stock consumption is
likewise delayed.

THE HOUSEHOLD INDUSTRY

Tho industries of finance (banking), manufacturing, and government, real counterparts of the pure industries of capital, goods, and services, are easily defined because they are generally logically structured. Because of this their processes can be described mathematically and their technical coefficients can be easily deduced. This, however, is not the case with the service industry known as the household industry.

HOUSEHOLD MODELS

When the industry flow diagram is represented by a 2-block system of households on the right and all other industries on the left, the following results.

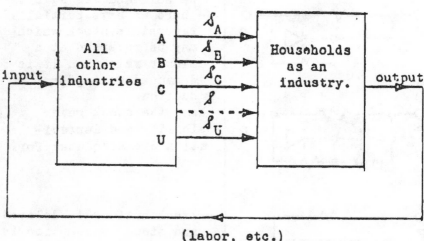

(labor, etc.)

The arrows from left to right labeled A, B, C, etc., denote flow of economic value from the industries in the left hand block to the industry in the right hand block called 'households'. These may be thought of as the monthly consumer flows of the following commodities. A- alcoholic beverages, B- beef, C- coffee,...., U- unknown, etc..

The problem which a theoretical economist faces is that the consumer preferences of any household is not easily predictable and the technical coefficients of any one household tend to be a non-linear, very complex, and variable function of income, prices, etc..

Computer information derived from the use of the universal product code in conjunction with credit card purchase as an individual household identifier could change this state of affairs. But the U.P.C. method is not yet available on a national or even a significant regional scale. To compensate for this data deficiency, an alternate indirect approach of analysis has been adopted known as economic shock testing. This method, widely used in the aircraft manufacturing industry develops an aggregate statistical sort of data.

Applied to economics, this means that all of the households in one region or in the whole nation are studied as a group or class rather than individually, and the mass behavior rather than individual behavior is used to discover useful estimates of the technical coefficients governing the economic structure of the hypothetical single household industry.

Notice in the industry flow diagram that the values for the flows A, B, C, etc., are accessible to measurement in terms of selling prices and total sales of commodities.

One method of evaluating the technical coefficients of the household industry depends upon shocking the prices of a commodity and noting the changes in the sales of all of the commodities.

ECONOMIC SHOCK TESTING

In recent times, the application of Operations Research to the study of the public economy has been obvious for anyone who understands the principles of shock testing.

In the shock testing of an aircraft airframe, the recoil impulse of firing a gun mounted on that

airframe causes shock waves in that structure
which tell aviation engineers the conditions under
which parts of the airplane or the whole airplane
or its wings will start to vibrate or flutter like
a guitar string, a flute reed, or a tuning fork,
and disintegrate or fall apart in flight.

Economic engineers achieve the same result
in studying the behavior of the economy and the
consumer public by carefully selecting a staple
commodity such as beef, coffee, gasoline, or sugar
and then causing a sudden change or shock in its
price or availability, thus kicking everybody's
budget and buying habits out of shape.

They then observe the shock waves which result
by monitoring the changes in advertising, prices,
and sales of that and other commodities.

The objective of such studies is to acquire
the know-how to set the public economy into a
predictable state of motion or change, even a controled self-destructive state of motion which will
convince the public that certain "expert" people
should take control of the money system and rees-
tablish security (rather than liberty and justice)
for all. When the subject citizens are rendered
unable to control their financial affairs, they
of course, become totally enslaved, a source of
cheap labor.

Not only the prices of commodities, but also
the availability of labor can be used as the means
of shock testing. Labor strikes deliver excellent
test shocks to an economy, especially in the
critical service areas of trucking (transportation),
communication, public utilities (energy, water,
garbage collection), etc..

By shock testing, it is found that there is
a direct relationship between the availability of
money flowing in an economy and the psychological
outlook and response of masses of people dependent
upon that availability.

For example, there is a measureable quanti-
tative relationship between the price of gasoline,
and the probability that a person would experience
a headache, feel a need to watch a violent movie,
smoke a cigarette, or go to a tavern for a mug of beer.

It is most interesting that, by observing and measuring the economic modes by which the public tries to run from their problems and escape from reality, and by applying the mathematical theory of Operations Research, it is possible to program computers to predict the most probable combination of created events (shocks) which will bring about a complete control and subjugation of the public, through a subversion of the public economy (by shaking the plum tree).

INTRODUCTION TO THE THEORY OF ECONOMIC SHOCK TESTING

Let the prices and total sales of commodities be given and symbolized as follows.

COMMODITIES	PRICE FUNCTION	TOTAL SALES
alcoholic beverages	A	S_A
beef	B	S_B
coffee	C	S_C
gasoline	G	S_G
sugar	S	S_S
tobacco	T	S_T
unknown balance	U	S_U

Let us assume a simple economic model in which the total number of important (staple) commodities are represented as beef, gasoline, and an aggregate of all other staple commodities which we will call the hypothetical miscellaneous staple commodity 'M'. (e.g., M is an aggregate of C, S, T, U, etc..)

EXAMPLE OF SHOCK TESTING

Assume that the total sales, P, of petroleum products can be described by the linear function of the quantities B, G, and M, which are functions of the prices of those respective commodities. Then

$$P = a_{PB} B + a_{PG} G + a_{PM} M$$

where B, G, and M are functions of the prices of beef, gasoline, and miscellaneous, respectively, and a_{PB}, a_{PG}, and a_{PM} are constant coefficients defining the amount by which each of the functions B, G, and M affect the sales, P, of petroleum products. We are assuming that B, G, and M are variables independent of each other.

If the availability or price of gasoline is suddenly changed, then G must be replaced by $G + \Delta G$. This causes a change in the petroleum sales from P to $P + \Delta P$. Also we will assume that B and M remain constant when G changes to $G + \Delta G$.

$$(P + \Delta P) = a_{PB} B + a_{PG}(G + \Delta G) + a_{PM} M.$$

Expanding this expression, we get

$$P + \Delta P = a_{PB} B + a_{PG} G + a_{PG} \Delta G + a_{PM} M$$

and subtracting the original value of P we get for the change in P

Change in $P = \Delta P = a_{PG} \Delta G$

Dividing by ΔG we get

$$a_{PG} = \frac{\Delta P}{\Delta G} .$$

This is a rate of change in P due only to an isolated change in G, ΔG.

In general, a_{jk} is the partial rate of change in the sales effect j due to a change in the causal price function of commodity k. If the interval of time were infinitesimal, this expression would be reduced to the definition of the total differential of a function, P.

For if $a_{jk} = \dfrac{\partial j}{\partial k}$, and if $P = a_{PB}B + a_{PG}G + a_{PM}M$

and B, G, and M are independent variables, then

$$a_{PB} = \frac{\partial P}{\partial B} \quad \text{and}$$

$$dP = \frac{\partial P}{\partial B}dB + \frac{\partial P}{\partial G}dG + \frac{\partial P}{\partial M}dM$$

Integrating, we get

$$P = \int \frac{\partial P}{\partial B}dB + \int \frac{\partial P}{\partial G}dG + \int \frac{\partial P}{\partial M}dM.$$

If the a_{jk} are constant coefficients, then the rates, $\partial j/\partial k$, are constant also and can be taken outside of the integrals. Therefore,

$$P = \frac{\partial P}{\partial B}\int dB + \frac{\partial P}{\partial G}\int dG + \frac{\partial P}{\partial M}\int dM \quad \text{or}$$

$$\boxed{P = \frac{\partial P}{\partial B}B + \frac{\partial P}{\partial G}G + \frac{\partial P}{\partial M}M + K.}$$

Furthermore,

$$\delta_A = \frac{\partial \delta_A}{\partial B}B + \frac{\partial \delta_A}{\partial G}G + \frac{\partial \delta_A}{\partial M}M + K_A$$

$$\delta_B = \frac{\partial \delta_B}{\partial B}B + \frac{\partial \delta_B}{\partial G}G + \frac{\partial \delta_B}{\partial M}M + K_B$$

$$\delta_C = \frac{\partial \delta_C}{\partial B}B + \frac{\partial \delta_C}{\partial G}G + \frac{\partial \delta_C}{\partial M}M + K_C$$

$$\delta_U = \frac{\partial \delta_U}{\partial B}B + \frac{\partial \delta_U}{\partial G}G + \frac{\partial \delta_U}{\partial M}M + K_U$$

38

When the price of gasoline is shocked, all of the coefficients with round G (∂G) in the denominator are evaluated at the same time. If B, G, and M were independent, and sufficient for description of the economy, then three shock tests would be necessary to evaluate the system.

There are other factors which may be represented the same way.

For example, the tendency of a docile sub-nation to withdraw under economic pressure may be given by

$$\phi = \frac{\partial \phi}{\partial G} G + \frac{\partial \phi}{\partial W_P} W_P + \cdots$$

where G is the price of gasoline, W_P is the dollars spent per unit time (referenced to say 1939) for war production during 'peace' time, etc.. These quantities are presented to a computer in matrix format as follows.

$$
\begin{vmatrix}
\dfrac{\partial P}{\partial G} & \dfrac{\partial P}{\partial B} & \cdots & \dfrac{\partial P}{\partial U} \\[2mm]
\dfrac{\partial F}{\partial G} & \dfrac{\partial F}{\partial B} & \cdots & \dfrac{\partial F}{\partial U} \\[2mm]
\cdots & \cdots & \cdots & \cdots \\[2mm]
\dfrac{\partial T}{\partial G} & \dfrac{\partial T}{\partial B} & \cdots & \dfrac{\partial T}{\partial U} \\[2mm]
\dfrac{\partial \phi}{\partial G} & \dfrac{\partial \phi}{\partial B} & \cdots & \dfrac{\partial \phi}{\partial U}
\end{vmatrix}
\cdot
\begin{vmatrix}
G \\ B \\ \cdot \\ \cdot \\ U
\end{vmatrix}
=
\begin{vmatrix}
P - K_P \\ F - K_F \\ \cdot \\ T - K_T \\ \phi - K_\phi
\end{vmatrix}
$$

$$\uparrow \qquad\qquad \uparrow$$
$$X_k \qquad\qquad Y_j$$

or $\begin{bmatrix} a_{jk} \end{bmatrix} \begin{bmatrix} X_k \end{bmatrix} = \begin{bmatrix} Y_j \end{bmatrix}$

where the a_{jk} are defined by $\qquad a_{jk} = \dfrac{\partial X_j}{\partial X_k}$.

and $\quad X_1 = G \qquad Y_1 = P - K_P$

$\qquad X_2 = B \qquad Y_2 = F - K_F$

$\qquad X_3 =$ etc. $\qquad Y_3 =$ etc.

Finally, inverting this matrix, i.e., solving for the X_k in terms of the Y_j, we get, say,

$$\left[b_{kj} \right] \left[Y_j \right] = \left[X_k \right] .$$

This is the result into which we substitute ϕ to get that set of conditions of prices of commodities, bad news on T.V., etc., which will deliver a collapse of public morale ripe for take over.

Once the economic price and sales coefficients a_{jk} and b_{kj} are determined, they may be translated into the technical supply and demand coefficients g_{jk}, c_{jk}, and $1/L_{jk}$.

Shock testing of a given commodity is then repeated to get the time rate of change of these technical coefficients.

INTRODUCTION TO
ECONOMIC AMPLIFIERS

Economic amplifiers are the active components
of economic engineering. The basic characteristic
of any amplifier (mechanical, electrical, or economic) is that it receives an input control signal
and delivers energy from an independent energy source
to a specified output terminal in a predictable
relationship to that input control signal.

The simplest form of economic amplifier is a
device called advertising.

If a person is spoken to by a T.V. advertiser
as if he were a twelve year old, then, due to
suggestability, he will, with a certain probability,
respond or react to that suggestion with the uncritical response of a twelve year old and will reach
into his economic reservoir and deliver its energy
to buy that product on impulse when he passes it in
the store.

An economic amplifier may have several inputs
and outputs. Its response might be instantaneous
or delayed. Its circuit symbol might be a rotary
switch if its options are exclusive, qualitative,
'go' or 'no go', or it might have its parametric
input/output relationships specified by a matrix
with internal energy sources represented.

Whatever its form might be, its purpose is to
govern the flow of energy from a source to an output
sink in direct relationship to an input control
signal. For this reason, it is called an active
circuit element or component.

Economic Amplifiers fall into classes called
strategies, and , in comparison with electronic
amplifiers, the specific internal functions of an
economic amplifier are called logistical instead
of electrical.

Therefore, economic amplifiers not only
deliver power gain, but also, in effect, are used
to cause changes in the economic circuitry.

In the design of an economic amplifier we must
have some idea of at least five functions, which are

(1) the available input signals,
(2) the desired output control objectives,

(3) the strategic objective,
(4) the available economic power sources,
(5) the logistical options.

The process of defining and evaluating these factors and incorporating the economic amplifier into an economic system has been popularly called game theory.

The design of an economic amplifier begins with a specification of the power level of the output, which can range from personal to national. The second condition is accuracy of response, i.e., how accurately the output action is a function of the input commands. High gain combined with strong feedback helps to deliver the required precision. Most of the error will be in the input data signal. Personal input data tends to be specific, while national input data tends to be statistical.

SHORT LIST OF INPUTS

Questions to be answered:

(1) what	(3) where	(5) why
(2) when	(4) how	(6) who

General sources of information:

(1) telephone taps	(3) analysis of garbage
(2) surveillance	(4) behavior of children in school

Standard of living by:

(1) food	(3) shelter
(2) clothing	(4) transportation

Social contacts:

(1) telephone - itemized record of calls
(2) family - marriage certificates, birth certificates, etc.
(3) friends, associates, etc.
(4) memberships in organizations
(5) political affiliation

THE PERSONAL PAPER TRAIL

Personal buying habits, i.e.,
Personal consumer preferences:

(1) checking accounts
(2) credit card purchases
(3) 'tagged' credit card purchases — the credit
    card purchase of products bearing the U.P.C.
    (Universal Product Code)

Assets:

(1) checking accounts   (5) automobile, etc.
(2) savings accounts   (6) safety deposit at bank
(3) real estate   (7) stock market
(4) business

Liabilities:

(1) creditors   (3) loans
(2) enemies (see - legal)   (4) consumer credit

Government sources (ploys)*:

(1) Welfare   (4) doles
(2) Social Security   (5) grants
(3) U.S.D.A. surplus food   (6) subsidies

Government sources (via intimidation)

(1) Internal Revenue Service
(2) OSHA
(3) Census
(4) etc.

* Principle of this ploy -- the citizen will
  almost always make the collection of information easy if he can operate on the 'free
  sandwich principle' of 'eat now, and pay later'.

Other Government sources -- surveillance of U.S.Mail.

HABIT PATTERNS -- PROGRAMING

Strengths and weaknesses:

(1) activities (sports, hobbies, etc.)
(2) see 'legal' (fear, anger, etc. - crime record)
(3) hospital records (drug sensitivities, reaction
    to pain, etc.)
(4) psychiatric records (fears, angers, disgusts,
    adaptability, reactions to stimuli, violence,
    suggestibility or hypnosis, pain, pleasure,
    love, and sex)

Methods of coping -- of adaptability -- behavior:

(1) consumption of alcohol   (5) other methods of
(2) consumption of drugs   escaping from
(3) entertainment   reality
(4) religious factors influencing behavior

Payment modus operandi (MO) -- pay on time, etc.:

(1) payment of telephone bills
(2) energy purchases (electric, gas,...)
(3) water purchases
(4) repayment of loans
(5) house payments
(6) automobile payments
(7) payments on credit cards

Political sensitivity:

(1) beliefs   (3) position   (5) projects/
(2) contacts   (4) strengths/weaknesses activities

Legal inputs - behavior control
  (Excuses for investigation search, arrest, or
  employment of force to modify behavior.)

(1) court records   (4) reports made to police
(2) police records -NCIC (5) insurance information
(3) driving record   (6) anti-establishment
                             acquaintances

NATIONAL INPUT INFORMATION

Business sources (via I.R.S., etc..):

(1) prices of commodities
(2) sales
(3) investments in
    (a) stocks/inventory
    (b) production tools and machinery
    (c) buildings and improvements
    (d) the stock market

Banks and credit bureaus:

(1) credit information
(2) payment information

Miscellaneous sources:

(1) polls and surveys
(2) publications
(3) telephone records
(4) energy and utility purchases

SHORT LIST OF OUTPUTS

Outputs – create controled situations.
--- manipulation of the economy, hence society.
--- control by control of compensation and income.
Sequence:
(1) allocates opportunities.
(2) destroys opportunities.
(3) controls the economic environment.
(4) controls the availability of raw materials.
(5) controls capital.
(6) controls bank rates.
(7) controls the inflation of the currency.
(8) controls the possession of property.
(9) controls industrial capacity.
(10) controls manufacturing.
(11) controls the availability of goods
(12) controls the prices of commodities.
(13) controls services the labor force etc..
(14) controls payments to government officials.
(15) controls the legal functions
(16) controls the personal data files – uncorrectable
     by the party slandered
(17) controls advertising.
(18) controls media content.
(19) controls material available for T.V. viewing.
(20) disengages attention from real issues.
(21) engages emotions.
(22) creates disorder, chaos, and insanity.
(23) controls design of more probing tax forms.
(24) controls surveillance.
(25) controls the storage of information.
(26) develops psychological analyses and profiles
     of individuals.
(27) controls legal functions (repeat of 15).
(28) controls sociological factors
(29) controls health options.
(30) preys on weaknesses.
(31) cripples strengths.
(32) leaches wealth and substance.

TABLE OF STRATEGIES

DO	TO, OR TO GET
Keep public ignorant.	less public organization
access to control points (prices, sales)	required reaction to outputs for feedback
Create preoccupation.	lower defenses
Attack the family unit.	control of the education of the young
Give them less cash and more credit and doles.	more self-indulgence and more data
Attack the privacy of the church.	destroy faith in this sort of government
social conformity	computer programing simplicity
Minimize the tax protest.	maximum economic data
	minimum enforcement problems
Stabilize the consent coefficients	simplicity
tight control of variables	simpler computer input data -- greater predictability
Establish boundary conditions	problem simplicity
	solution of differential and difference equations.
proper timing	less data snift and blurring.
minimum resistance to control	maximum control
maximize control	ultimate objective
collapse of currency	destroy the faith of the American people in each other
END	

DIVERSION,
THE PRIMARY STRATEGY

Experience has proven that the simplest method of securing a silent weapon and gaining control of the public is to keep the public undisciplined and ignorant of basic systems principles on the one hand, while keeping them confused, disorganized, and distracted with matters of no real importance on the other hand.

This is achieved by:

(1) disengaging their minds, sabotaging their mental activities, by providing a low quality program of public education in mathematics, logic, systems design, and economics, and by discouraging technical creativity

(2) engaging their emotions, increasing their self-indulgence and their indulgence in emotional and physical activities, by:

    (a) unrelenting emotional affrontations and attacks (mental and emotional rape) by way of a constant barrage of sex, violence, and wars in the media – especially the T.V. and the newspapers.

    (b) giving them what they desire – in excess --- 'junk food for thought' -- and depriving them of what they really need

(3) rewriting history and law and subjecting the public to the deviant creation, thus being able to shift their thinking from personal needs to highly fabricated outside priorities.

These preclude their interest in and discovery of the silent weapons of social automation technology.

The general rule is that there is profit in confusion; the more confusion, the more profit. Therefore, the best approach is to create problems and then offer the solutions.

48

DIVERSION SUMMARY

MEDIA: Keep the adult public attention diverted
away from the real social issues, and
captivated by matters of no real importance.

SCHOOLS: Keep the young public ignorant of real
mathematics, real economics, real law,
and real history.

ENTERTAINMENT: Keep the public entertainment below
a sixth grade level.

WORK: Keep the public busy, busy, busy, with no
time to think; back on the farm with the
other animals.

CONSENT,
THE PRIMARY VICTORY

A silent weapon system operates upon data
obtained from a docile public by legal (but not
always lawful) force. Much information is made
available to silent weapon systems programers
through the Internal Revenue Service.(See Studies
in the Structure of the American Economy for an
I.R.S. source list.) This information consists
of the enforced delivery of well organized data
contained in federal and state tax forms collected,
assembled, and submitted by slave labor provided
by taxpayers and employers. Furthermore, the
number of such forms submitted to the I.R.S. is a
useful indicator of public consent, an important
factor in strategic decision making. Other data
sources are given in the Short List of Inputs.

Consent Coefficients -- numerical feedback indi-
cating victory status. Psychological basis:
When the government is able to collect tax
and seize private property without just compensation, it is an indication that the public is
ripe for surrender and is consenting to enslavement
and legal encroachment. A good and easily quanti-
fied indicator of harvest time is the number of
public citizens who pay income tax despite an
obvious lack of reciprocal or honest service from
government.

AMPLIFICATION ENERGY SOURCES

The next step in the process of designing an economic amplifier is discovering the energy sources. The energy sources which support any primitive economic system are, of course, a supply of raw materials, and the consent of the people to labor and consequently assume a certain rank, position, level, or class in the social structure; i.e.,to provide labor at various levels in the pecking order.

Each class, in guaranteeing its own level of income, controls the class immediately below it, hence preserves the class structure. This provides stability and security, but also government from the top.

As time goes on and communication and education improve, the lower class elements of the social labor structure become knowledgeable and envious of the good things that the upper class members have. They also begin to attain a knowledge of energy systems and the ability to enforce their rise through the class structure.

This threatens the sovereignty of the elite.

If this rise of the lower classes can be postponed long enough, the elite can achieve energy dominance,and labor by consent no longer will hold a position of an essential economic energy source.

Until such energy dominance is absolutely established, the consent of people to labor and let others handle their affairs must be taken into consideration, since failure to do so could cause the people to interfere in the final transfer of energy sources to the control of the elite.

It is essential to recognize that at this time, public consent is still an essential key to the release of energy in the process of economic amplification.

Therefore, consent as an energy release mechanism will now be considered.

LOGISTICS

The successful application of a strategy requires a careful study of inputs, outputs, the strategy connecting the inputs and the outputs, and the available energy sources to fuel the strategy. This study is called logistics.

A logistical problem is studied at the elementary level first, and then levels of greater complexity are studied as a synthesis of elementary factors.

This means that a given system is analyzed, i.e., broken down into its sub-systems, and these in turn are analyzed, until, by this process, one arrives at the logistical 'atom', the individual.

This is where the process of synthesis properly begins, and at the time of the birth of the individual.

THE ARTIFICIAL WOMB

From the time a person leaves its mother's womb, its every effort is directed toward building, maintaining, and withdrawing into artificial wombs, various sorts of substitute protective devices or shells.

The objective of these artificial wombs is to provide a stable environment for both stable and unstable activity: to provide a shelter for the evolutionary processes of growth, and maturity - i.e., survival; to provide security for freedom and to provide defensive protection for offensive activity.

This is equally true of both the general public and the elite. However, there is a definite difference in the way each of these classes go about the solution of problems.

THE POLITICAL STRUCTURE OF A NATION
-DEPENDENCY-

The primary reason why the individual citizens of a country create a political structure is a subconscious wish or desire to perpetuate their own dependency relationship of childhood.

Simply put, they want a human god to eliminate
all risk from their life, pat them on the head, kiss
their bruises, put a chicken on every d'nner table,
clothe their bodies, tuck them into bed at night,
and tell them that everything will be alright when
they wake up in the morning.

This public demand is incredible, so the human
god, the politician, meets incredibility with incredibility by promising the world and delivering
nothing. So who is the bigger liar?, the public?,
or the 'godfather'?

This public behavior is surrender born of fear,
laziness, and expediency. It is the basis of the
welfare state as a strategic weapon, useful against
a disgusting public.

ACTION/OFFENSE

Most people want to be able to subdue and/or
kill other human beings which disturb their daily
lives, but they do not want to have to cope with
the moral and religious issues which such an overt
act on their part might raise. Therefore, they
assign the dirty work to others (including their
own children) so as to keep the blood off their
own hands. They rave about the humane treatment
of animals and then sit down to a delicious ham-
burger from a whitewashed slaughterhouse down the
street and out of sight. But even more hypocriti-
cal, they pay taxes to finance a professional
association of hit men collectively called politicians, and then complain about corruption in
government.

RESPONSIBILITY

Again, most people want to be free to do things
(to explore, etc.) but they are afraid to fail.

The fear of failure is manifested in irrespon-
sibility, and especially in delegating those personal responsibilities to others where success is
uncertain or carries possible or created liabilities
(law) which the person is not prepared to accept.

They want authority (root word - 'author'),
but they will not accept responsibility or liability.

So, they hire politicians to face reality for them.

SUMMARY

The people hire the politicians so that the people can:

(1) obtain security without managing it.
(2) obtain action without thinking about it.
(3) inflict theft, injury, and death upon others without having to contemplate either life or death.
(4) avoid responsibility for their own intentions.
(5) obtain the benefits of reality and science without exerting themselves in the discipline of facing or learning either of these things.

They give the politicians the power to create and manage a war machine to:
(1) provide for the survival of the NATION/WOMB.
(2) prevent encroachment of anything upon the NATION/WOMB.
(3) destroy the enemy who threatens the NATION/WOMB.
(4) destroy those citizens of their own country who do not conform for the sake of stability of the NATION/WOMB.

Politicians hold many quasi-military jobs, the lowest being the police which are soldiers, the attorneys and the C.P.A.s next who are spies and saboteurs (licensed), and the judges who shout the orders and run the closed union military shop for whatever the market will bear. The generals are industrialists. The 'presidential' level of commander-in-chief is shared by the international bankers. The people know that they have created this farce and financed it with their own taxes (consent), but they would rather knuckle under than be the hypocrit.

Thus, a nation becomes divided into two very distinct parts, a DOCILE SUB-NATION and a POLITICAL SUB-NATION. The political sub-nation remains att-ached to the docile sub-nation, tolerates it, and leaches its substance until it grows strong enough to detach itself and devour its parent.

SYSTEM ANALYSIS

In order to make meaningful computerized economic decisions about war, the primary economic flywheel, it is necessary to assign concrete logistical
values to each element of the war structure --
personnel and materiel alike.

This process begins with a clear and candid
description of the sub-systems of such a structure.

THE DRAFT
(As military service.)

Few efforts of human behavior modification are
more remarkable or more effective than that of the
socio- military institution known as the draft. A
primary purpose of a draft or other such institution
is to instill, by intimidation, in the young males of
a society the uncritical conviction that the government is omnipotent. He is soon taught that a prayer
is slow to reverse what a bullet can do in an in-
stant. Thus, a man trained in a religious environment for eighteen years of his life can, by this
instrument of the government, be broken down, be
purged of his fantasies and delusions in a matter of
mere mouths. Once that conviction is instilled,
all else becomes easy to instill.

Even more interesting is the process by which
a young man's parents, who purportedly love him, can
be induced to send him off to war to his death.
Although the scope of this work will not allow this
matter to be expanded in full detail, nevertheless,
a coarse overview will be possible and can serve to
reveal those factors which must be included in some
numerical form in a computer analysis of social and
war systems.

We begin with a tentative definition of the
draft.

The draft (selective service, etc.) is an
institution of compulsory collective sacrifice
and slavery, devised by the middle aged and the
elderly for the purpose of pressing the young

54

into doing the public dirty work. It further
serves to make the youth as guilty as the elders,
thus making criticism of the olders by the youth
less likely (Gcnerational Stabilizer). It is
marketed and sold to the public under the label
of "patriotic➖national" service.

Once a candid economic definition of the draft
is achieved, that definition is used to outline the
boundaries of a structure called a Human Value System,
which in turn is translated into the terms of game
theory. The value of such a slave laborer is given
in a Table of Human Values, a table broken down into
categories by intellect, experience, post service
job demand, etc..

Some of these categories are ordinary and can be
tentatively evaluated in terms of the value of certain jobs for which a known fee exists. Some jobs are
harder to value because they are unique to the demands of social subversion, for an extreme example:
the value of a mother's instruction to her daughter
causing that daughter to put certain behavioral
demands upon a future husband, ten or fifteen years
hence, thus, by suppressing his resistance to a
perversion of a government, making it easier for a
banking cartel to buy the State of New York in, say,
twenty years.

Such a problem leans heavily upon the observations and data of wartime espionage and many types of
psychological testing. But crude mathematical models
(algorithms, etc.) can be devised, if not to predict,
at least to predetermine these events with maximum
certainty. What does not exist by natural cooper-
ation is thus enhanced by calculated compulsion.
Human beings are machines, levers which may be
grasped and turned, and there is little real difference between automating a society and automating
a shoe factory.

These derived values are variable. (It is
necessary to use a current Table of Human Values for
computer analysis.) These values are given in true
measure rather than U.S. dollars, since the latter
is unstable, being presently inflated beyond the

production of national goods and services so as to
give the economy a false kinetic energy ('paper'
inductance).

The silver value is stable, it being possible
to buy the same amount with a gram of silver today as could be bought in 1920. Human value
measured in silver units changes slightly due to
changes in production technology.

ENFORCEMENT

FACTOR I

As in every social system approach, stability
is achieved only by understanding and accounting
for human nature (action/reaction patterns). A
failure to do so can be, and usually is, disastrous.

As in other human social schemes, one form or
another of intimidation (or incentive) is essential
to the success of the draft. Physical principles
of action and reaction must be applied to both
internal and external sub-systems.

To secure the draft, individual brainwashing/
programing and both the family unit and the peer
group must be engaged and brought under control.

FACTOR II   FATHER

The man of the household must be house-broken
to ensure that junior will grow up with the right
social training and attitudes. The advertising media,
etc., are engaged to see to it that father-to-be is
pussy-whipped before or by the time he is married.
He is taught that he either conforms to the social
notch cut out for him or his sex life will be hob-
bled and his tender companionship will be zero. He
is made to see that women demand security more than
logical, principled, or honorable behavior. By the
time his son must go to war, father (with jelly for
a back bone) will slam a gun into junior's hand before father will risk the censure of his peers, or
make a hypocrit of himself by crossing the investment he has in his own personal opinion or self-
esteem. Junior will go to war or father will be
embarrassed. So junior will go to war, the true
purpose of the war notwithstanding.

FACTOR III MOTHER

The female element of human society is ruled by
emotion first and logic second. In the battle between logic and imagination, imagination always wins,
fantasy prevails, maternal instinct dominates so that
the child comes first and the future comes second.
A woman with a newborn baby is too starry-eyed to
see a wealthy man's cannon fodder or a cheap source
of slave labor. A woman must, however, be conditioned
to accept the transition to "reality" when it comes,
or sooner.

As the transition becomes more difficult to
manage, the family unit must be carefully disintegrated, and state controled public education and
state operated child care centers must become more
common and legally enforced so as to begin the de-
tachment of the child from the mother and father at
an earlier age. Inoculation of behavioral drugs
can speed the transition for the child (mandatory).
CAUTION: A woman's impulsive anger can override her
fear. An irate woman's power must never be underestimated, and her power over a pussy-whipped
husband must likewise never be underestimated.
It got women the vote in 1920.

FACTOR IV JUNIOR

The emotional pressure for self-preservation
during time of war and the self-serving attitude of
the common herd that have an option to avoid the
battlefield -- if junior can be persuaded to go --
is all of the pressure finally necessary to propel
Johnny off to war. Their quiet blackmailings of
him are the threats: "No sacrifice, no friends;
no glory, no girlfriends."

FACTOR V SISTER

And what about junior's sister? She is given
all the good things of life by her father, and
taught to expect the same from her future husband
regardless of the price.

FACTOR VI CATTLE

Those who will not use their brains are no
better off than those who have no brains, and so
this mindless school of jellyfish, father, mother,
son, and daughter, become useful beasts of burden
or trainers of the same.

9 781585 093809